Blend Phonics

Lessons and Stories

A Complete Phonics Reading Program

For All Ages

by

Donald L. Potter

ISBN: 1481802011
ISBN-13: 978-1481802017

www.donpotter.net

DEDICATED TO

MRS. HAZEL LOGAN LORING

Whose 1980 publication of
Reading Made Easy with Blend Phonics for First Grade
made it possible for **every** teacher
to be successful teaching
every student to read.

CONTENTS

Acknowledgments

ACKNOWLEDGMENTS

To Mrs. Elizabeth Brown for writing the wonderful Blend Phonics Stories for her Blend Phonics' students and mine.

To Dr. George González of Edinburg University, McAllen, TX, for his Eight Comprehension Powers Method, that I referred to when creating the comprehension questions.

To Mr. Ray Laurita for helping me understand the Levels of Word Processing Difficulty, and the importance of perceptual maturity in order to avoid the development of a confused visual patterning response. He also alerted me to the dangers of teaching sight-words before students have mastered basic phonics.

To Miss Geraldine Rodgers for helping me understand the existence of two kinds of readers (*objective* versus *subjective*) based on how they were initially taught (*from the sounds* versus *from the meaning*).

To Dr. Ronald P. Carver for teaching me the importance of spelling as the best means for teaching students to read fluently.

To my many tutoring students whose suggestions helped me improve the program, as they worked through it to improve their reading.

To Pat Lent and Lloyd Loring, Hazel Loring's children, for permission and encouragement to publish their mother's program as a commercial venture in order to reach a larger audience than the free e-book (pdf), that I published in late 2003, has been able to reach. The free e-book is still available on my website, www.donpotter.net

To Bob Sweet of the National Right to Read Foundation for his 1996 essay, "A Century of Miseducation of American Teachers," where I first learned of the existence of Mrs. Loring's 25 page phonics booklet.

Blend Phonics
Lessons and Stories

Step 1

Short Vowels and Single-Letter Consonants

Units 1 – 5
Stories 1 - 7

b	b	b	c	c	c	c	d
ba	ba	ba	ca	ca	ca	ca	da
bat	bag	bad	can	cap	cab	cat	dad

f	f	g	h	h	h	j	l
fa	fa	ga	ha	ha	ha	ja	la
fan	fat	gas	hat	ham	had	jam	lap

l	m	m	m	n	p	p	p
la	ma	ma	ma	na	pa	pa	pa
lad	map	man	mat	nap	pan	pad	pat

qu	r	r	r	r	s	s
qua	ra	ra	ra	ra	sa	sa
quack	rat	ran	rag	rap	sap	sad

S	t	t	v	w	y	t
Sa	ta	ta	va	wa	ya	ta
Sam	tag	tap	van	wag	yak	tax

w	z	a	a	a
wa	za	am	an	at
wax	zag			

Sam, a cat

Story 1, Unit 1

bat bag bad can cap cab cat dad fan fat
gas hat ham had jam lap lad map man
mat nap pan pad pat quack rat ran rag
rap sap sad Sam tan tag tap van wag yak
ax tax wax am an at Ann lass mass pass
zag [a]

Sam, a cat

Sam sat. Sam and Nan sat. Nan can pat
Sam.

<u>Answer these questions</u>.

1. Is Nan a cat?
2. What did Sam do?
3. What can Nan do to Sam?
4. Do you have a cat?

<u>Spell these words</u>: bat, bag, can, cap, fan, fat, map, pan, pad, am,
at, rag, quack, van.

A Tin Can

bib bin bit bill big dim dip fib fit fin hit
hip him hill hid jig kiss kid kill lip lid
miss mill mix nip pit in pig pill quick
rib rim rid sit sip sin tip tin Tim vim
win wig will yip zig fig rip it if rig fix
zigzag his is did six

A Tin Can

Fill a tin can. Dip a lid. Mix a fig in a
tin can. Win a tin can.

Answer these questions.

1. What is to be filled?
2. Dip a what?
3. What do we do with a fig?
4. What do we win?

Spell these words: bib, bin, fit, bill, him, lip, kiss, miss, pig, sip,
tin, wig, win, mix.

5

A Mop

Story 3, Unit 3

bob bog cot cob dog doll dot Don fog
got hot hop hod job lot log mob mop
nod not pod pop pot rob rot rod sop sob
sod tot top hog on off box fox boss loss
moss toss

A Mop

Hop on a mop, not on a top. A mop
cannot sob. A mop got off a box.

Answer these questions.

1. Do you hop on a mop or a top?
2. Tell me what a mop cannot do?
3. A mop got off a _____.
4. Can you use a mop to comb your hair?

Spell these words: pod, pop, rod, sob, sod, hog, on, off, fox, bob,
fog, mob, log, not.

A Bug

Story 4, Unit 4

bud bug bun bus but cub cuff cup cut duck dug fun fuss gull gum gun Gus hug hum hut jug lug mud muff mug muss nut pup rub rug run sum sun tub up us

A Bug

A bug cut up a muff. Can a bug hum? Can a bug hug? A bug can hug a jug and a cub.

<u>Answer these questions</u>:

1. What can a bug hug?
2. Have you ever heard a bug hum?
3. Would you hug a bug?
4. What do you call a little bear?

<u>Spell these words</u>: bug, but, bud, gun, jug, fuss, fun, cup, hum, duck, muff, nut, tub, lug.

A Wet Hen

Story 5, Unit 5

bed beg bell bet dell den fed fell get hen
jet let leg less men mess met net peg
pen pet red sell set Ted tell ten vet web
well wet yell yes yet

A Wet Hen

A hen got fed in a pen. A hen fell in a
cup. A hen got wet, a wet mess.

Answer these questions:

    1. Where did a hen get fed?
    2. The hen fell into a _____.
    3. What happened to a hen when it fell in a cup?
    4. Can a hen lay an egg?

Spell these words: bet, bell, bed, jet, hen, men, met, leg, let, red,
set, web, well, yes.

A Pug

Story 6, Unit 5 Review

get got gut net Nat nit nut not rot rut rat rod rid red set sit sat tell till beg bag bog bug big box hen ham hum him hem peg pig pug Ted Todd tad bet bit bat but bed bid bud bad lit lot let fed fad fat fit jet jot jut pet pot pit pat putt wax pen pin pun pan web wed wet wit up us

A Pug

Nat got a hip pug. A pug is a dog. A pug sat on a bag in a bog. A pug fell in a bog — sad, wet pug.

Answer these questions:

1. On what did the pug sit?
2. Is a bog wet or dry?
3. How did a pug feel when he fell?
4. Who got a hip pug?

Spell these words: get, got, nit, bog, big, peg, pug, bad, fed, pit, jazz, pet, wit, wet, us.

9

A Fox

Story 7, Unit 5 Review

dell dull doll dill bill bell Bill hill hull
fell fill full fox fax fix well will den
Dan din Don less lass loss vet vat men
man mom mum sell sill mess mass miss
moss muss mop map muff miff mutt
mat met mitt Mat ten tin tan tax tux keg
kiss kid kit cad cod sod cup cop cap cog
sap sop sup sip zigzag quick quack

A Fox

A quick fox can fix a fax and a box. A
fox wed a dog. A fox and a dog will sit
in a den.

Answer these questions:

    1. What two things can a fox fix?
    2. Whom did a fox wed?
    3. Where will the fox and dog sit?
    4. What is a den?

Spell these words: mop, man, met, sad, sup, sit, less, lass, loss,
mess, moss, miss, sell.

Blend Phonics
Lessons and Stories

Step 2

Consonant Blends and Consonant Digraphs

Units 6 – 15
Stories 8 - 21

The Lamp

band bent bend belt bump camp damp
desk fast fist felt fond fund gift tilt gust
hand hint jump just lend land lamp
hump lift list lint melt must milk mist
mend pump pant quest rest rust sent
send silk next sand tent test went wind
and ask best its

duck Jack kick lock luck lick neck pick
quick quack rock sick tack

The Lamp

Will Max mend (fix) a lamp? A lamp will sit
in a silk tent. Pick up a lamp quick and lift it
off a pump.

<u>Answer these questions</u>:

    1. What does mend mean?
    2. Where does a lamp sit?
    3. How fast do we need to pick up a lamp?
    4. Pick the lamp off the _____.

<u>Spell these words</u>: band, hand, fast, lamp, send, melt, must, hump, went,
rock, kick.

Ship on a Shelf

Story 9, Unit 7

cash dish fish hush wish

shall shed shelf ship shop shot shut

Ship on a Shelf

Tim's mom set a gift box on a shelf in a shed. It had a fast ship in it. His mom had his dad get it at a shop.

Answer these questions:

    1. What was in the gift box on the shelf?
    2. Where did Tim's mom set the gift box?
    3. Was the ship fast or slow?
    4. Where did Tim's dad go to get the ship?

Spell these words: cash, dish, shut, ship, shed, shop, shall, hush.

The Thump

Story 10, Unit 8

<u>th</u>an that them this thus [the]

thick thin thud thump bath with

The Thump

Did that thump? Shad felt the big thump. THUMP! Not a bump, but a big, big thump. Thus, this is a thump. A thump, a big thud.

<u>Answer these questions</u>:

    1. What is a thump?
    2. Make a thumping sound for me.
    3. Who felt the big thump?
    4. Was it as bump or a thump?

<u>Spell these words</u>: bath, thump, them, this, thick, thin, with, than.

The Chick

Story 11, Unit 9

chat chin chill chick chop chip chum much rich such

catch ditch fetch latch match notch patch pitch witch thatch – mechanic

The Chick

The rich chick sat in a ditch. The chick got such a shock—a pitch got in the ditch, a big pitch. The chick can not catch the pitch.

Answer these questions:

1. Where did the rich chick sit?
2. Can you pitch a ball?
3. Was it as big or little pitch?
4. Can the chick in the ditch catch the pitch?

Spell these words: chat, chin, chip, chick, chop, rich, such, catch, ditch, match, witch.

The Whisk

Story 12, Unit 10

want was water watch

what when which whiff whip whisk

The Whisk

Ron can whisk up water with a rag, just watch. Rick can watch him whisk up the water with the rag. What a fast whisk that was! It went whip, whip.

Answer these questions:

    1. Did you know that to whisk is to do something quickly?
    2. Who can whisk up the water?
    3. Who can watch Ron whisk up the water?
    4. Should people whisk up spilled water?

Spell these words: want, was, water, watch, what, when, whip, whisk.

Sing a Song

Story 13, Unit 11

bang gang hang rang sang ding
Ping-Pong ring sing thing-a-ling wing
king thing gong long song hung lung
rung sung

Sing a Song

Sing a sad song; sing a long, sad song.
Nan sang a sad song. The king can bang
a gong. The gong will sing a long gong
song.

Answer these questions:

    1. Is the song happy or sad?
    2. Is the song long or short?
    3. Who sang the song?
    4. Who banged the gong?

  Spell these words: bang, sung, long, thing, rang, bang, sing, sang, wing, ring, gong.

The Tank

Story 14, Unit 12

bank bunk dunk kink link mink pink rink sink tank sank chunk thank honk think

The Tank

The pink tank can honk. The tank sank in the sink. It had a dunk in the sink, I think

Answer these questions:

    1. Does the tank have a horn?
    2. Where did the tank sink?
    3. What color was the tank?
    4. Do you still play with toys in the sink?

Spell these words: honk, rink, pink, tank, think, sank, link, bank, dunk.

The Flag

Story 15, Unit 13

blush black block blend bland bliss
blink   clip clap click cliff clock clink
clank clinch clench cling clang club
flash flesh flip flap fling flung flit flat
flag flock fled flop   glad glass gland
plan plant plop plot pluck plum plus
scat scan scuff scum scalp scotch
skin skip skid skill sketch

The Flag

The flag sat flat in the club. It did not flap
and flit in the sun. The flag was sad. In a
blink, Skip had a plan. Skip flung the flag in
the sun. The flag was glad. Thanks, Skip!

Answer these questions:

    1. Why was the flag sad?
    2. Who flung the flag in the sun?
    3. Where was the flag at first?
    4. Where was the flag at the end?

Spell these words: black, blink, clap, cling, club, glass, skin, scalp,
flip, flash, fling.

The Sled

Story 16, Unit 13

slush slot slum slap slam slash slip sled
smack smelt smug smash   snip snob
snap snug snuff snub   spun spot spill
spell spank spunk spin span spat spit
stuck stop still stem stand step stub stab
stuff stiff   swim swell swam swift
switch swing swept [to]

The Sled

The sled slid and spun—it was stuck, bad luck.
Stan went to swing the sled up, but it was still
stuck, bad luck. The sled was in a bad spot. Stan
swept up the sled with a quick slash. Smash!
Crash! The sled spun and slid off the spot. It was
not stuck. It was swept off with a clink and a
clank. Stan can sled, what fun!

Answer these questions:
1. Who pulled the sled?
2. What happened to the sled?
3. The sled was in a bad _____.
4. Have you ever sled on a snow sled?

Spell these words: slush, slap, slip, snap, snug, stop, stand, step, swim,
swing, switch.

The Brass Band

Story 17, Unit 14

brag brand brass brim brick bring branch brush

crab crash cramp crack crib crop crunch crust

drag drank drop drum drink dress drunk drip drug

The Brass Band

The brass band got me up with a crash, a bang, and a crack.

Crack! Bang! Crash!

The drum went bang.

Crash! Bang!

Answer these questions:

1. What woke up the author?
2. What sound did the drum make?
3. Name one instrument in a brass band?
4. Would you like to play in a band?

Spell these words: brag, brick, crab, cramp, crop, crack, bring, branch.

The Frog

Story 18, Unit 14

Fran Frank frost frump fresh French
Fred frog frock
grand grass grasp grant gruff grip grunt
grin   prank press prim print
track trap trick trim trip trot truck trend
trust [he]

The Frog

The trim frog was slim. The trim frog
had a fresh bug, yum! With a grin, the
frog pressed a bug on a French fish. (It
was a prank, I trust.)

Answer these questions:

1. Was the trim, slim Frog skinny?
2. Was the bug fresh or nine days old?
3. Show me a big grin.
4. Have your ever played a prank on anyone?

Spell these words: grand, fresh, frog, grant, grass, grin, grip, press,
print, truck, trap.

Yum and Yuck

Story 19, Unit 15

Divide between 2 consonants: bed-rock, nap-kin

bedrock napkin flapjack hubcap
landmass blacktop Midland helmet
shipment laptop catfish kidnap hotdog
bobcat upland humbug rabbit puppet
dental husband sunset sudden combat
traffic pocket lesson Hobbit magnet
tiptop catnap catnip nutmeg upon

Yum and Yuck

A rabbit bit in a hotdog. Yuck! Then, the
rabbit bit a flapjack, yum! It has nutmeg in
it, yum, yum, yum in the tum tum! A bobcat
can nip on the hotdog.

Answer these questions:

1. Did the rabbit like the hotdog?
2. Did the rabbit like the flapjack?
3. What did the flapjack have in it?
4. Can a bobcat nip on a hotdog?

Spell these words: hubcap, laptop, catfish, hotdog, pocket, husband,
sunset, rabbit.

The Hilltop

Story 20, Unit 15

Divide between 2 consonant sounds:
ash-can, egg-nog, back-stop

ashcan eggnog backstop cashbox
trashcan hilltop

The Hilltop

The hilltop sang in the sunset. It had
bedrock up on the tiptop; it was a strong
hilltop. It was not humbug.

Answer these questions:

   1. Do hilltops really sing?
   2. Was it singing at sunup or sunset?
   3. What did the hill have on the tiptop?
   4. A humbug is a hoax. What is another
      word for hoax? Ask your teacher if you don't know.

Spell these words: hilltop, cashbox, backstop, trashcan, humbug.

Handstands

Story 21, Unit 15

Divide before and after consonant blends:
chest-nut, sun-spot

chestnut sunspot handcuff sandbag
dishpan gumdrop endless dogsled
dustpan desktop handbag wingspan
filmstrip handstand

Handstands

Trish can flip up in a handstand. Was it
an endless handstand? Well, it was a
long handstand, but not endless.

Answer these questions:

    1. Who can do handstands?
    2. How long is endless?
    3. Would you like to do a handstand?
    4. Do they teach handstands at your school?

Spell these words: sandbag, dishpan, endless, handbag, desktop,
handstand.

Blend Phonics
Lessons and Stories

Step 3

Long Vowel VCE Words
Long o endings: -old, -ost, -oll, olt, -oth,
Long i endings: -ild, -ind
Short words with long final vowel

Units 16 – 18
Stories 22 – 27

Short to Long Vowel Practice
with Final Silent e

cap-cape	past-paste	gap-gape
rat-rate	pan-pane	back-bake
fad-fade	Sam-same	mad-made
lack-lake	snack-snake	quack-quake
at-ate	hat-hate	tap-tape
pin-pine	rip-ripe	dim-dime
lick-like	Tim-time	kit-kite
bit-bite	fill-file	rid-ride
pill-pile	sit-site	mill-mile
not-note	cop-cope	mop-mope
rob-robe	hop-hope	dot-dote
cut-cute	tub-tube	us-use
purr-pure	duck-duke	cub-cube
pet-Pete	met-mete	

Cakes

Story 22, Unit 16

ate bake cake came cane cape case date daze fade fake fate game gate gave gaze haste hate haze lake lame late made make mane mate name pale pane paste quake rake rate safe sake same save take tame taste vase wake waste chase shake shame blame blaze brake brave crate crave craze drape flake flame glade grape grave plane snake stake trade

Cakes

Shane can bake a lame cake. It shakes and quakes. It tastes yum, but it lacks fame. Shane made it, but can Shane make a not fake cake? Shane got help, and then Shane did bake a cake that was not lame. Shane ate it at a game. It was a big hit!

Answer these questions:
1. Who baked the cake?
2. What was wrong with the cake?
3. Did Shane get help to bake a cake that would make a hit?
4. Where did Shane eat the cake?

Spell these words: bake, cake, ate, date, made, shake, tame, save, grape, trade, safe.

The Kite

here these Pete

bite dime dine bike dike fine fife dive
file five hide hive lime life like mine
mite mile nine pike pine pile quite kite
ride shine side spike smile slime stile
swine spine ripe time tile tide wife wine
slide pipe size glide while white drive
pride prime prize

The Kite

Pete made a fine kite. The kite will ride
up five miles! Pete smiled with pride.
Pete's kite was quite a prize.

Answer these questions:

1. Who made the kite?
2. What kind of kite did he make?
3. How high will the kite fly?
4. Why did Pete smile?

Spell these words: here, dime, bite, life, dine, mile, ride, kite, size, drive, side, wife.

Pine Cones

bone cone cope code dote dole dome globe hole home hope joke lone lode lope poke pole quote rode robe rope sole spoke slope smoke note tone tote stole mope mole vote woke broke drove probe

Pine Cones

These pine cones fell at Mike's home. A man stole nine pine cones as a bad joke. Mike moped, and then Mike spoke to the man. The man was sad that Mike moped. Mike spoke to the man. Then the man gave the pine cones back. With a smile, he spoke, "Here, take a tote bag. Stick the pine cones in a tote bag and quit moping."

Answer these questions:

1. Where did the pine cones fall?
2. Why was Mike sad?
3. Does anyone you know mope when they are sad?
4. Do you know that a tote is a little bag?

Spell these words: bone, cone, home, lone, rope, rode, note, mope, broke, drove.

The Rude Duke

Story 25, Unit 16

cube duke dune cute tube tune mule flute prune rule rude plume brute use

The Rude Duke

A rude Duke sat in a hut. The Duke ruled a glade. The Duke woke up mad and spoke rude things. The Duke was a brute.

Answer these questions:

    1. Where did the rude Duke live?
    2. Was the Duke nice to people?
    3. Was the Duke happy or mad when he woke up?
    4. Should a Duke be rude to people?

Spell these words: cube, duke, cute, tune, plume, use, rule, rude, brute, flute.

The Cold

Story 26, Unit 17

bold old cold fold gold hold mold sold
told scold colt jolt molt bolt volt   both
toll roll most post host   child wild mild
blind find kind mind rind wind [who]

The Cold

It was cold. The wet got hold; then it
got cold, cold, cold. It was not mild. It
was just cold. Who likes cold? Not this
child!

<u>Answer these questions</u>:

    1. Was it cold and wet?
    2. Did the child like the wet cold?
    3. Do you like the cold?
    4. Do you have a warm jacket?

<u>Spell these words</u>: bold, cold, gold, sold, colt, volt, toll, roll, most,
child, wild, find.

Go!

Story 27, Unit 18

be he me we she the

go no so going

Go

He can go. She can go. We can go. Go fast, so fast, just go, go, go! He will be going. She will be going. We will not fold. We will not scold. Just go, just go, just go.

Answer these questions:

    1. Can he go?
    2. Can she go?
    3. Are they going fast or slow?
    4. Should we scold?

Spell these words: go, we, she, the, me, no, so, going, he.

Blend Phonics
Lessons and Stories

Step 4

R-Controlled Vowels

Units 19 – 21
Stories 28 - 31

The Car

Story 28, Unit 19

bar barn car chart charm darn dark far farm hard harm jar lark mark mart park part spark smart scar star tar start warm

The Car

The dark black car sat parked on a farm. It had spark plugs that did not go, so the car did not run. With a spark plug fix, it will run like a charm.

Answer these questions:

1. What color was the car?
2. Where was the car parked?
3. Tell me some farm animals.
4. What did they fix on the car?

Spell these words: bar, car, charm, dark, far, farm, hard, mark, park, star, start, spark.

Morning on the Farm

Story 29, Unit 20

born cord cork corn for fork fort horn
horse pork porch scorn scorch storm
stork torn torch morn morning worn

Morning on the Farm

It's morning on the farm. A stork and a
horse will be born. Both will munch on
corn. Oh, no, a storm! The stork and
the horse can be warm on the porch or
in the barn.

<u>Answer these questions</u>:

1. What is the weather like in the story?
2. Is it evening, afternoon, or morning?
3. What two animals will be born?
4. Can they be warm?

<u>Spell these words</u>: for, cork, born, horse, horn, corn, stork, worn,
pork.

The World

Story 30, Unit 21

clerk fern jerk her herd term after never
bird birth dirt fir first girl sir stir third
curb burn fur hurt purr turn word world
work worm [of]

The World

God made a lot of things in the world.
He made girls, ferns, birds, dirt, and
cats that purr.

<u>Answer these questions</u>:

1. According to the story, who made the world?
2. What sound do cats make?
3. How big do you think the world is?
4. What do cats like to eat?

<u>Spell these words</u>: her, bird, dirt, sir, girl, burn, fur, turn, word,
world, work.

Can I be?

camper cutter catcher chopper dipper drummer helper jumper marker farmer pitcher under planner runner sitter starter swimmer sender spinner better

actor doctor janitor visitor

Can I be?

We can be drummers, helpers, farmers, runners, janitors, or doctors. Then, rest and be a sitter, but first work, then sit.

Answer these questions:

   1. What do you want to be when you grow up?
   2. Which do you do first, sit or work?
   3. Why do we have to sit sometimes?
   4. Do you get to rest at school?

Spell these words: camper, drummer, farmer, helper, under, better, doctor, visitor.

Blend Phonics
Lessons and Stories

Step 5

Vowel Digraphs and Diphthongs

Units 22 – 35
Stories 32 - 49

A Fine Day

Story 32, Unit 22

ail bail brain fail gain grain jail maid
mail paid aid pain rail rain sail tail train
wait wail

bay clay day play gray hay jay lay may
pay pray ray say sway way

A Fine Day

I say, what a fine day! A jaybird lay on
the grain and ate. He had a long tail.
The mail came with a play train for a
child. We can sail on the bay on this
fine day. Stay and play.

Answer these questions:

1. What had kind of day was it?
2. What kind of bird was eating grain?
3. Was his tail short or long?
4. What came in the mail?

Spell these words: rain, brain, grain, mail, sail, tail, day, hay, jay,
say, pray, may, way.

A Bee

Story 33, Unit 23

bee beef beech beet deed breeze fee feet
feed feel free freeze fleet green greet
heed heel jeep keep keen peep reed see
seed seen seem sleep sleeve sleet sweep
sweet sheep meet need wee weed week
weep three queen

A Bee

I see a bee go on the breeze. It lay on a
green weed. Then it went to greet a
reed. If it gets cold, the bee will hide in
a hive and keep warm.

Answer these questions:

    1. On what was the bee going?
    2. On what was the bee lying?
    3. What will the bee do if it gets cold?
    4. Do you like honey?

Spell these words: bee, see, seed, feel, feet, keep, free, three, weed,
meet, seen, need.

The Sea

Story 34, Unit 24

beat beach beast bean cream cheat
cheap deal dream feast east each leaf
leap leave lean meal least sea tea teach
reach read real eat each near

The Sea

I dream and think near the sea. I can eat a
peach on the beach. I just drink tea and eat a
peach, but I dream that I eat a feast. A feast
on the beach near the sea - fine indeed!

Answer these questions:

    1. What two things did the author do by the sea?
    2. What did the author have for a feast?
    3. How much food do you eat at a feast?
    4. Have you ever had a feast by the sea?

Spell these words: beat, bean, cream, eat, read, sea, tea, dream,
east, leaf, each.

Bread of Life

Story 35, Unit 24

bread breath dead death health instead read threat tread wealth weather

steak break great bear

The Bread of Life

Bread of Life is wealth indeed; it keeps me in health, not death. Bread of Life – life instead of death.

Answer these questions:

    1. What is wealth?
    2. Is bread good for your health?
    3. Why is it called, "Bread of Life?"
    4. What is your favorite bread?

Spell these words: bread, read, health, tread, steak, break, great, bear.

Pie

Story 36, Unit 25

cried cries dried dries fried fries lie lies lied pie pies spies tie tied tried

Pie

She makes fine pies. He who lies or cries will not get pie. She made fried pies; at least she tried.

"Flies, do not eat the pies!" she cried.

<u>Answer these questions</u>:

    1. What kind of pies does she make?
    2. Do liars get to eat her pie?
    3. Do criers get to eat her pies?
    4. What does she think of flies on pies?

<u>Spell these words</u>: cried, cries, fried fries, lie, lies, pie, pies, tie, tied.

The Chief Priest

Story 37, Unit 25

brief chief grief field priest relief believe yield belief [give]

The Chief Priest

Do not give the Chief Priest grief. He can help thee see and believe and find relief. Belief comes for those that yield.

<u>Answer these questions</u>:

    1. How can the Chief Priest help?
    2. To whom does belief come?
    3. Is seeing believing?
    4. Have you ever felt grief?

<u>Spell these words</u>: brief, chief, field, believe, relief, priest.

Sunny Day

Story 38, Unit 26

army candy cubby daddy dolly dusty
funny gummy party happy handy hilly
healthy fairly fifty messy penny puppy
rainy sunny sleepy thirty twenty silly
wealthy pretty [are]

The Sunny Day

Sunny day! Daddy likes a sunny day,
but he dislikes a rainy day. Twenty
sunny days are fairly dandy, fifty makes
him happy.

Answer these questions:

    1. Which day does the daddy dislike?
    2. Do you like rainy days?
    3. What do you like to do on a rainy day?
    4. How many days make dad happy?

Spell these words: army, dolly, daddy, funny, happy, puppy,
penny, pretty.

The Fly

Story 39, Unit 26

by cry dry fly my myself

ply sly try sky shy why

The Fly

"Do not cry, my shy fly," I cried.

"But," spoke the fly, "I can not stay dry, so much water in the sky."

"Why," replied I, "A fly can stay dry, just try; find a spot under a pig sty." The fly tried, and he got dry, by and by.

Answer these questions:

    1. Did the fly like water?
    2. Where was the water?
    3. How did the fly stay dry?
    4. Can flies really talk?

Spell these words: by, cry, dry, my, myself, ply, sly, try, sky, shy, why.

Goat and Toad

Story 40, Unit 27

boat boast coat coach coast goat float
load loaf road soap toad throat roast
soapy foe goes hoe hoed Joe toe toes
woe

Goat and Toad

A goat and a toad hoed a big garden. It
was hot, hard work to hoe in the sun.

"Woe, woe," moaned the toad.

"Woe, woe, hoe, hoe," moaned the
goat. The goat and toad sat in the shade
and drank water. The water felt sweet
and wet on the throat.

Answer these questions:

   1. What were goat and toad doing in the garden?
   2. Why do you think they were hoeing?
   3. Where did they sit to drink water?
   4. How did the water taste?

Spell these words: boat, coat, goat, road, soap, hoe, Joe, toe, doe.

The Fish Bowl

Story 41, Unit 28

bow bowl blow crow glow grow grown growth flow low row slow tow throw show shown snow fellow follow pillow willow yellow own [they]

The Fish Bowl

The fish bowl sits on a low shelf. Six fish swim fast, three go slow. How slow will they go? A bit slow, they just go with the flow. Seven fish are yellow; the other fellow, he's white like snow.

Answer these questions:

    1. Where is the fish bowl?
    2. Do all the fish swim fast?
    3. Are there any yellow fish?
    4. How white is snow?

Spell these words: bowl, blow, grow, flow, low, row, yellow, pillow, snow.

Brown Cow

Story 42, Unit 29

cow crowd clown crown brown drown
frown flower gown growl howl power
powder row now town bow down

The Brown Cow

The brown cow cannot growl or howl.
Now it can frown and go to town, but it
cannot growl or howl.

Answer these questions:

    1. Name two things the brown cow can do?
    2. Why do people frown?
    3. What sound does a cow make?
    4. Do brown cows give brown milk?

Spell these words: cow, down, town, now, brown, flower, power,
clown, crown.

A Mouse

Story 43, Unit 29

cloud found ground house loud mound out our mouse pound round sound shout scout

you   country young   soul

A Mouse

You may not want to see a mouse. A child may shout out "Eek!" with a loud shout at a mouse. We hope we will not see a mouse in the house.

Answer these questions.

    1. Do we want to see a mouse in the house?
    2. Why did the child shout at the mouse?
    3. What do we hope?
    4. Should a mouse be in a house?

Spell these words: loud, our, found, mouse, round, sound, you.

Boys

Story 44, Unit 30

boy boys joy joys toy toys oyster
oysters

boil coin join joint oil soil spoil
point toil loin [do]

Boys

Most boys like toys. Most boys do not
like oysters boiled in oil. Boys find joy
in play joined with soil.

Answer these questions:

    1. What do most boys like?
    2. I like oysters. Do you like them?
    3. What is a game that you play on the soil?
    4. What is another word for soil?

Spell these words: boy, joy, toy, boys, toys, boil, coin, join, oil,
point, toil.

Loose Stoop

Story 45, Unit 31

boot booth coo cool boost droop food groom goose doom moon roof loose room proof mood gloom noon soon roost stool stoop spoon spool shoot too tool tooth troop coolness zoo cooler foolish smooth teaspoon noonday toothbrush scooter papoose tooting school pool fool

The Loose Stoop

We had a loose stoop, which tried to doom us; but do not gloom, we fixed it with a tool. Now, it's safe to roost on the stoop and rest and stay cool.

Answer these questions:

1. Did you know that stoop is a porch with steps in front of a house or other building?
2. Have you ever set on a stoop?
3. Gloom is when you feel dark and sad. Have you ever felt gloom?
4. Is it safe now to sit on the stoop?

Spell these words: food, moon, room, noon, soon, spook, stoop, too, pool, school, tooth.

A Good Book

Story 46, Unit 32

book booklet cook crook brook cooker
good foot footstep hoof hook hood look
looking soot took stood shook wool
wood wooden woolen footstool

A Good Book

A good book can teach you how to
cook, how to chop wood, or how to fish
in a brook. I like a good book. It can
help you look at the world better.

Answer these questions:

    1. What are some things a good book can teach you?
    2. What is your favorite book?
    3. How can a good book help you look at the world
       better?
    4. Would you like to write a book someday?

Spell these words: book, cook, good, foot, hook, soot, took, wool,
wood, stood.

Dawn

Story 47, Unit 33

crawl crawling drawn fawn hawk jaw law pawn paw saw shawl thaw yawn draw

cause clause faun haul fault pause

Dawn

Dawn broke. I saw a fawn crawl out of the woods. Up in the sky, I saw a hawk fly by. I paused and yawned, my jaw just had to yawn. Dawn is nice, but it is hard not to yawn at dawn.

Answer these questions:

1. Is dawn early morning or late evening?
2. What kind of animal is a hawk?
3. Do you yawn at dawn?
4. Why do you think the dawn is nice?

Spell these words: crawl, crawling, drawn, yawn, paw, law, saw, draw, cause, haul, fault.

A Ball

Story 48, Unit 34

already almost also bald false halt malt salt ball call mall wall fall small tall hall stall

A Ball

You can throw a ball at a wall or a goal. It's hard to halt a fast ball. In many ball games, it helps to be tall. Also, it helps not to fall, unless you fall and grab the ball.

Answer these questions:

1. Halt is another word for stop. Why is it hard to halt a fast ball?
2. What is your favorite ball game?
3. Why would a basketball player want to be tall?
4. Do you play ball with anyone?

Spell these words: all, fall, ball, bald, halt, also, stall, mall, tall, wall, small.

Stew

blew brew chew crew drew grew flew
threw dew few mew new news pew
stew
blue clue flue glue true due hue Sue

Stew

I smell stew. Yum, yum! But, I must
wait and let it brew. Any news yet on
my stew? I cannot wait to chew and
chew, I hope it will not taste like glue.
Sue calls out, "Time for stew!" It's true
blue food, not yucky goo. Yippee, stew!

Answer these questions:

1. Is stew real food?
2. Who called out, "Time for stew?"
3. Was the stew ready yet?
4. Do you like stew?

Spell these words: blew, crew, few, new, stew, clue, true, due,
blue.

Blend Phonics
Lessons and Stories

Step 6

Advanced Spelling Patterns

Units 36 – 47
Stories 50 - 62

Asleep

Story 50, Unit 36

a about adrift afar ajar alike ahead amuse around arouse apart aside asleep astir awake awhile away

Asleep

The house sleeps. I alone am awake, not a thing, not a mouse astir. I look around and see a door ajar, but still not a mouse astir. I amuse myself awhile then go to bed. At last, asleep!

Answer these questions:

1. What do astir and ajar mean?
2. Was the mouse making noise?
3. Is it important to get enough sleep?
4. Do you like a good story before going to sleep?

Spell these words: a, about, afar, ajar, alike, amuse, aside, asleep, awake, away.

The Bush

Story 51, Unit 37

careful pull bull full push bush
fullback fulfill put

The Bush

I put a bush in our yard, but now it's too
big. I must pull the bush out, but I must
be careful not to step on my plants or
pull out my back. I wish I had not put
in that bush.

Answer these questions:

1. What is the matter with the bush?
2. What does the author have to do now?
3. Why does he write, "Be careful?"
4. Have you ever done something you wished you hadn't done?

Spell these words: pull, bull, full, push, bush, put, careful.

The Circus

Story 52, Unit 38

cent cell cease center civil cinder
cyclone circus cinch cigar acid cistern
ace brace chance decide dance dunce
face fleece fence France hence ice lace
mice nice niece pace place peace piece
prance prince pencil price race rice
space slice spice since twice thence
choice voice   special sugar

The Circus

A special circus came to town. They did a
dance about France. They also had a silly
clown race in the center ring. The price was
nice. The last act had mice balance on a
fence.

Answer these questions:
1. Have you ever seen a circus?
2. What was the dance about?
3. Where did the silly clown race take place?
4. What was the last act?

Spell these words: cent, ice mice, nice, face, pace, rice, race, place.

The Stage

Story 53, Unit 39

age barge chance cage engage fringe
huge large lunge hinge page plunge
rage range sage stage wage urge budge
bridge badge dodge edge fudge hedge
lodge nudge pledge ledge judge ridge
smudge wedge ginger giraffe gist giblet
gyp gypsy gymnast garage

The Stage

We saw a play on a huge stage. The stage fit a
whole barge (a big flat bottom boat) that is extra
large. The play had a gymnast and a gypsy stuck
in a cage on the barge. The gymnast lunged up on
a bridge, then pulled the gypsy up to a ledge. The
gymnast's feat saved the day. Hurray!

Answer these questions:

1. Where was the play?
2. How big was the stage?
3. Who were stuck in the cage?
4. Who saved the day?

Spell these words: age, large, cage, page, wage, rage, fudge, judge,
edge, badge.

68

The Flight

Story 54, Unit 40

bright high blight tight might slight
thigh fight flight fighter night right
plight sigh sight light moonlight
taught caught daughter
gh = f: rough tough laugh laughter
laughing enough

The Flight

I might like to make a high flight. I'd fly at
night and see the moonlight and see how
bright the stars can shine. I'd laugh and
hope that I was not caught in a tree; that
plight might make me sigh. But, oh, it
might be nice to fly high up in the sky.

Answer these questions:

1. When can we see the moonlight?
2. Can planes fly at night?
3. Have you ever been in a plight?
4. Do you think it would be nice to fly?

Spell these words: high, light, right, night, plight, fight, sight,
taught, rough, laugh.

69

The Knight

Story 55, Unit 41

knee kneel knelt knight knife knit knot know known knock   chasten glisten hasten listen often soften   wreath wretch write wrist wring wrote wreck wrong answer sword comb climb debt doubt dumb lamb limb thumb   calf half walk   hour honor honest ghost

The Knight

The brave knight went out to face a dragon with only a sword. He walked around a lake, went across a dark forest, and climbed up a tall hill to face the beast. He hastened on his way, listening often to check for danger. At last, he found the dragon, and he knocked him down with only one blow. His story has been written of often. Just listen, it will be told and known far and wide.

1. What did the brave knight go out to face?
2. Did the knight have a gun?
3. What was the knight listening for?
4. Would you like to fight a dragon?

Spell these words: knee, knife, knight, often, listen, write, wrote, half, walk, hour, honest.

Cheese, Please!

Story 56, Unit 42

choose chose cheese ease because noise
nose pause pose praise please rose rise
tease these those wise as has is

Cheese, Please!

What is it you choose to eat?

"Cheese, please," they replied.

I paused a bit and rose to get closer. "What did
you say, there was a lot of noise?"

"**Cheese, please!**" they shouted in reply.

With a smile, I teased, "Leaves, you say, you
can't eat leaves."

"No, **Cheese, please!**" they shouted forth.

"Oh, Cheese, you say, why didn't you say so
before?"

Answer these questions:

    1. What did they choose to eat?
    2. What did the waiter think he said?
    3. Was the waiter just teasing?
    4. What is your favorite flavor of cheese?

Spell these words: choose chose, ease, please, nose, noise, rose,
rise, has, is, as.

The Elephant

Story 57, Unit 43

elephant nephew orphan prophet pamphlet photograph phonograph phone telephone telegraph alphabet phonics

The Elephant

I had an elephant. I got him a telephone, but he did not like the cord, so I got him a cell phone. He never called, so I got him a camera. He never took a photograph, so I got him a phonograph. It was quite a sight to see my elephant dance! Maybe I will teach him the alphabet and phonics next. He is a smart pet, even if he never calls.

Answer these questions:

1. Why didn't the elephant like the telephone?
2. Did the elephant use the camera?
3. What is a phonograph? If you don't know, ask your teacher?
4. Have you seen an elephant dance?

Spell these words: phone, phonics, telephone, elephant, orphan, prophet, alphabet.

My Mission

Story 58, Unit 44

battle bundle bottle buckle circle little middle pickle sample handle puzzle scramble scribble sprinkle struggle tickle wiggle   attention action addition affection invitation foundation education mention partition portion station section

expression impression mission

My Mission

My mission is to battle for a good education, one with good attention to phonics and addition. My invitation to you is to take action in this struggle and help restore the true foundation of education.

Answer these questions:

1. Name the two things to which we should pay good attention.
2. What is a mission?
3. Does everyone need an education?
4. Have you ever received an invitation?

Spell these words: bottle, circle, little, action, station, addition, mission, education.

Almost Finished

Story 59, Unit 45

ed Sounds Like short ĕd

added acted counted crowded ended folded landed
lighted painted planted printed rested waited

ed Sounds Like 'd

aimed burned called changed filled named saved
rained rolled stayed turned whaled

ed Sounds Like 't

baked boxed camped hitched picked hoped
hopped jumped liked looked packed pitched
stopped wished.   [your, have]

Almost Finished

We are almost finished! But, your education is not
ended. We have saved many things you have not yet
learned. Spelling, math, grammar, and history: an endless
list packed with mystery. I wish you well on your quest
to learn and change and reach your best.

Answer these questions:

    1. What do you want to be when you grow up?
    2. Have you enjoyed learning to read?
    3. What is your favorite subject I school?
    4. Would you like to become a teacher?

Spell these words: added, rested, saved, called, named, baked,
wished, liked.

The Slimy Spider

Story 60, Unit 46

baker racer shady lady caper paper favor
maker taper vapor savor wafer fatal nasal
taker label pacer halo fever cedar hero legal
regal before tidy slimy viper libel limy cider
spider tiger vital final tiny

oval grocer grocery oral open bony pony
donor solar holy clover focal local vocal
total sober over tulip lunar mural rural lucid
Lucy tyrant tyro

The Slimy Spider

The slimy spider climbed over the wall. I
screamed loudly, but the spider did not favor to
reply. He had an oval body that turned my legs to
jelly. I'd rather face down a tiger than a slimy
spider. So, I told the spider, "See ya later," and
left the spider on the wall.

Answer these questions:
1. What did the spider climb over?
2. What shape was the spider's body?
3. Which animal did the author fear most, a spider or a tiger?
4. Would you like a pet spider?

Spell these words: baker, maker, spider, slimy, tiny, solar, lunar,
rural, shady, tiger.

The Giant Ruin

Story 61, Unit 46

dial giant trial vial pliant crier brier drier poem poet poetry cruel duel fuel gruel ruin

The Giant Ruin

I ran through the brier patch, sighted a giant ruin. I hope it wasn't a cruel trick. I crept forward for a better look and saw that it was indeed a ruin. What might it be? A castle, a fortress, a palace perhaps.

Alas, it was just an old stone barn. But for my friends and I, that ruin was everything we dreamed. We fought many a battle and rescued many a princess in that lovely giant ruin.

Answer these questions:

1. Where was the author running?
2. What is a ruin?
3. The ruin was a stone _____.
4. Who did they rescue?

Spell these words: dial, trial, giant, poem, poet, poetry, fuel, ruin, cruel, crier.

Buried Treasure

Story 62, Unit 47

37 Dolch List Sight Words with "other" spelling patterns
and three words with the sound /zh/

do to today together two who into come done does
some one once of from again said could would
any many only are carry eight have give their they
very where were every been buy don't your

measure pleasure treasure

Buried Treasure

Jim and Terry met together today at Mark's house
to hunt for eight chests of buried treasure from the
dread pirate Blackbeard. Each chest is full of gold
beyond measure that is too heavy for two boys to
carry. Mark said he was very sure the treasure had
been put into one deep hole where there were
some bushes that could have many sharp stickers.
They said that it would be a great pleasure to give
every piece of gold to their dad, who could buy
any car with it.

Jim asked Mark, "When does your dad come
home again?"

Mark answered, "I don't know for sure. Not till
his work is done." The boys are going to dig and
dig and only stop once they find it.

<u>Answer these questions</u>:

    1. What are the three boy's names?
    2. What are they trying to find?
    3. What do they plan to do with the gold?
    4. Would you like to hunt for buried treasure?

<u>Spell these words</u>: do today two who into come done some one of said could many are eight have give their they very where were every been buy don't your treasure

Note from Internet Publisher: Donald L. Potter

I would like to thank Mrs. Elizabeth Brown for writing these little decodable stories to go with Hazel Loring's 1980 *Reading Made Easy with Blend Phonics for First Grade*. Mrs. Brown sent me the stories back in February of 2010 to use with my *Blend Phonics* students. I added the questions and spelling words on December 19, 2011. Mrs. Brown's phonics website is www.thephonicspage.org.

The stories add spice and interest to the task of learning to read with phonics. In order to avoid development of the inaccurate whole-word reading reflex, it is crucial for student to learn to decode **before** reading from connected text, Mrs. Brown has wisely included the phonics lessons **just before** the stories. This makes the program completely self-contained in this single book.

I added Unit 46 to teach the long vowel open syllable spelling pattern since there were no words with that spelling pattern in the original *Reading Made Easy for First Grade Blend Phonics.* It is interesting that many beginning phonics programs neglect to teach this common and important spelling pattern.

Unit 47 introduces the thirty-seven Dolch List Service Words that were not explicitly taught in the original *Blend Phonics* and three words with the /zh/ sound.

It is important to discuss the stories with the students to help them develop their ability to recall and understand what they read. I have added some sample comprehension questions at the end of the each story to encourage the development of attention and recall.

Notice that the stories are **decodable** rather than predictable. We do not use pictures because we believe they tend to encourage context guessing in beginning readers. Our goal is eliminate guessing, not encourage it. Twelve words introduced out of phonics sequence are included in the word lists in brackets. They should be taught with spelling before reading the story.

As a useful supplement to any phonics program, Mr. Potter has found the two Phonovisual Charts (Consonants and Vowels) very helpful in teaching the sound-to-symbol correspondences. www.phonovisual.org

A special thanks goes to my many tutoring students, who helped me detect errors and make various and sundry improvements to the program.

There are 2,307 running words in the *Blend Phonics Stories*.

Last edited for KDP Publishing on June 3, 2020.

Uppercase Alphabet Tapping Exercise
Automatic Letter Name Recognition

A   B   C   D

E   F   G

H   I   J   K

L   M   N   O   P

Q   R   S

T   U   V

W   X   Y   Z

Lowercase Alphabet Tapping Exercise
Automatic Letter Name Recognition

a   b   c   d

e   f   g

h   i   j   k

l   m   n   o   p

q   r   s

t   u   v

w   x   y   z

Key Words for Single-Letter Consonant Sounds

b	<u>b</u>at	p	<u>p</u>o<u>p</u>
c = k	<u>c</u>at	qu = kw	<u>qu</u>ack
c = s	<u>c</u>ent	s = s	<u>s</u>and
d	<u>d</u>ad	s = z	bell<u>s</u>
f	<u>f</u>an	t	<u>t</u>en<u>t</u>
g = g	<u>g</u>as	v	<u>v</u>an
g = j	<u>g</u>em	w	<u>w</u>ax
h	<u>h</u>at	x = ks	ta<u>x</u>
j	<u>j</u>am	x = gz	e<u>x</u>ist
l	<u>l</u>ap	x = z	<u>X</u>avier
m	<u>m</u>ap	y	<u>y</u>ak
n	<u>n</u>et	z	<u>z</u>oo

Consonant Digraphs: Two-Consonants – One Sound

sh	<u>sh</u>ip	ng	ki<u>ng</u>
ch	<u>ch</u>in	nk	ba<u>nk</u>
wh	<u>wh</u>eel	zh	mea<u>s</u>ure
<u>th</u>	<u>th</u>is	ck	du<u>ck</u>
th	<u>th</u>ing	ph	<u>ph</u>one

sh = ti, si: na<u>ti</u>on, occa<u>si</u>on

Key Words for Vowel Sound-to-Letter Correspondences

Long Vowel Sounds

1. /ā/: c<u>a</u>k<u>e</u>   d<u>ay</u>   p<u>ai</u>d   <u>eigh</u>t   b<u>ear</u>   b<u>a</u>-ker
2. /ē/: h<u>ere</u>   tr<u>ee</u>   m<u>ea</u>t   ch<u>ie</u>f   bab<u>y</u>   b<u>e</u>   f<u>e</u>-ver
3. /ī/: k<u>i</u>te   b<u>y</u>   t<u>ie</u>   l<u>igh</u>t   t<u>i</u>-ger
4. /ō/: h<u>o</u>le   b<u>oa</u>t   t<u>oe</u>   n<u>o</u>   <u>o</u>-val
5. /ū/: r<u>u</u>le,   f<u>ew</u>   bl<u>ue</u>   t<u>u</u>-lip

Short Vowels

6. /ă/: b<u>a</u>g
7. /ĕ/: b<u>e</u>g   br<u>ea</u>d
8. /ĭ/: b<u>i</u>g
9. /ŏ/: b<u>o</u>g   w<u>a</u>ter
10. /ŭ/: b<u>u</u>g   <u>a</u>m<u>o</u>ng

Other Vowel Sounds

11. /au/: s<u>aw</u>   f<u>au</u>lt   <u>a</u>ll   t<u>a</u>lk
12. /ar/: c<u>ar</u>
13. /Long o͞o/:   sp<u>oo</u>n
14. /Short o͝o/:   f<u>oo</u>t   p<u>u</u>t
15. /ou/: c<u>ow</u>   s<u>ou</u>th
16. /oi/: t<u>oy</u>   b<u>oi</u>l
17. /or/: f<u>or</u>k
18. /ur/: h<u>er</u>   f<u>ir</u>st   n<u>ur</u>se   doct<u>or</u>

Phonovisual Charts Correlation

Picture Keys for Teaching
the Sound-to-Symbol Correspondences

Unit 1: -a- (c<u>a</u>t), b (<u>b</u>ear), c (<u>k</u>ey), d (<u>d</u>uck), f (<u>f</u>an), g (<u>g</u>oat) h (<u>h</u>orn), j (<u>j</u>ar), k (<u>k</u>ey), l (<u>l</u>eaf), m (<u>m</u>onkey), n (<u>n</u>est), p (<u>p</u>ig), qu (<u>qu</u>een), r (<u>r</u>abbit), s (<u>s</u>aw), t (<u>t</u>op), v (<u>v</u>alentine), w (<u>w</u>agon), x (bo<u>x</u>), y (<u>y</u>ard), z (<u>z</u>ebra), ck (<u>k</u>ey).

Unit 2: -i- (f<u>i</u>sh), **Unit 3:** -o- (t<u>o</u>p), **Unit 4:** -u- (d<u>u</u>ck), **Unit 5:** -e- (b<u>e</u>d),

Unit 7: sh (<u>sh</u>ip), **Unit 8:** *th*, th (<u>th</u>ree & <u>th</u>is), **Unit 9:** ch/tch (<u>ch</u>erry),

Unit 10: wh (<u>wh</u>eel), **Unit 11:** -ng (swi<u>ng</u>), **Unit 12:** -nk (swi<u>ng</u>/ba<u>nk</u>),

Unit 16: a-e, e-e, i-e, o-e, u-e (c<u>a</u>ke, tr<u>ee</u>, f<u>i</u>ve, r<u>o</u>se, m<u>u</u>le),

Unit 17: -old, -olt, -oll, -ost, -oth (r<u>o</u>se), -ild, -ind (f<u>i</u>ve),

Unit 18: -o, -e (r<u>o</u>se , tr<u>ee</u>), **Unit 19:** ar (c<u>ar</u>), **Unit 20:** or (f<u>or</u>k),

Unit 21: er/ir/ur/or (f<u>ur</u>), **Unit 22:** ai/ay (c<u>a</u>ke), **Unit 23:** ee (tr<u>ee</u>),

Unit 24: ea (tr<u>ee</u>, b<u>e</u>d, c<u>a</u>ke), **Unit 25:** ie (f<u>i</u>ve, tr<u>ee</u>),

Unit 26: --y = ē, -y = ī (tr<u>ee</u>, f<u>i</u>ve), **Unit 27:** oa, oe (r<u>o</u>se),

Unit 28: ōw/ow (r<u>o</u>se, c<u>ow</u>), **Unit 29:** ou/ōu (c<u>ow</u>, r<u>o</u>se),

Unit 30: oy/oi (b<u>oy</u>), **Unit 31:** oo (m<u>oo</u>n),

Unit 32: oo (b<u>oo</u>k), **Unit 33:** aw/au (s<u>aw</u>), **Unit 34:** al/all (s<u>aw</u>),

Unit 34: ew/eu (m<u>u</u>le), **Unit 35:** a = ŭ (d<u>u</u>ck), **Unit 37:** ul/ull/ush (b<u>oo</u>k)

Unit 38: c = s, s = sh (<u>s</u>aw, <u>sh</u>ip), **Unit 39:** g = j (<u>j</u>ar),

Unit 40: gh (f<u>i</u>ve, s<u>aw</u>, <u>f</u>an), **Unit 42:** se = z (<u>z</u>ebra),

Unit 43: ph = f (<u>f</u>an), **Unit 44:** le (<u>l</u>eaf); tion, sion (<u>sh</u>ip),

Unit 46: ā, ē, ī, ō, ū, (c<u>a</u>ke, tr<u>ee</u>, f<u>i</u>ve, r<u>o</u>se, m<u>u</u>le)

SAMPLE PHONOVISUAL CHARTS

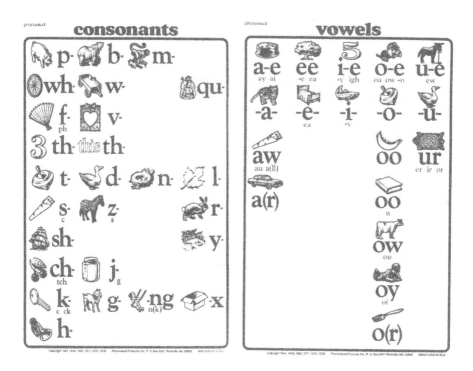

Explanation of Scientific Organization of Charts

Consonant Chart: The top of the chart starts at the front of the mouth and goes to the back going down the column. The first column (p, wh, f, th, t, s, sh, ch, k, h) are unvoiced consonants (Quiet Cousins). The second column (b, w, v, th, d, z, j g) represents voiced consonants (Noisy Cousins). The third column (m, n, ng) are nasals (Singing Cousins). The column on the right represents liquid consonants (qu, l, r, y, x).They related to the consonants to the left according to points of articulation (Neighbors).

Vowel Chart: Top row are long vowels spellings. Second row are short vowel spellings. The vowels below the short vowel row are called "other vowels." The small print represents secondary spellings.

Color Coded Large Wall Charts, Small Student Charts, and Flashcards can be ordered from www.phonovisual.org. They are a useful aid to teaching the sound-to-symbol correspondences.

WHY TEACH BLEND PHONICS?

By HAZEL LORING

It is my belief that most reading failures are caused by the perfectly normal and very common tendency of many children to look at words from right to left. That this tendency is neither abnormal nor pathological is evident by the fact that many languages are written from right to left: Hebrew, Arabic, etc. Before the time of Homer, Greek inscriptions were written in the bustrophedon (pathway of the ox) form: one line from left to right; the next line from right to left. Oriental languages are written in a vertical manner. There is no "physiologically correct" or incorrect direction in which a language may have been developed.

When a child sees a word as a whole he or she has no way of knowing in which direction it should be looked at until the correct direction is shown. Each child will look at it in whatever direction his/her tendencies dictate. If the word is in English and the child looks at it from right to left, he/she is in BIG TROUBLE: "ten" is not the same as "net"; "pat" is not the same as "tap" and if instead of "fun" some children see "nuf" they are headed toward confusion.

It has been common practice to teach the word as a whole in the first grade and, then, later in second grade, to introduce phonics in the form of word analysis. That is, the child is expected to break down the whole word into its component parts and thus deduce the relationship between phonemics (sounds) and graphemes (symbols).

This method can be reasonably successful if the child has a natural left to right tendency, is capable of deductive reasoning, and has memorized the whole word accurately. But what of the children of equal or even superior intelligence who have a natural right to left tendency? They cannot deduce correct phoneme/grapheme relationships because they are working from a false premise when they see the whole word in a reversed order. Even though they may have 20/20 vision, they do not see what the teacher sees in the expected order. They hear the phonemes in a left to right order, while seeing the graphemes from right to left – or perhaps in a confused – direction. This explains why some people think of word analysis as "phony phonics," and why the confused child is thought to have a learning disability or "dyslexia."

To be fair, although most techniques in word analysis are useless for the children with directional problems – or may even add to the confusion – there is one technique that may be helpful, i.e., that of teaching of the initial consonant as part of the whole word. As long as care is taken to be sure that each child looks at the *first* letter in the word as the sound is heard, the child will be able to learn the consonant sound. BUT THIS IS NOT ENOUGH. They must be able to learn the vowel sounds and it is imperative that they be given early directional training.

I have a daughter who for more than eleven years has taught remedial reading in an urban adult education institute. High school graduates, who have diplomas but who cannot read on a second grade level, come to her for tutoring. She tells me that most of them know the consonant sounds, but they cannot learn to read until after they have had training in blend phonics.

Directional guidance is inherent in the system of blend phonics. First we show the student the initial consonant in isolation and teach its sound. (True, we cannot pronounce the pure sound in isolation but must add a neutral vowel – or schwa – sound. However, this is of no importance because the schwa sound will be elided when we make the blend.) Next we show the student the vowel grapheme and teach its sound. *Then we blend the two sounds together* before adding the next consonant. There is no way for the child to go except from left to right, and with enough practice an automatic left to right habit is acquired. Then, to insure comprehension, it has been my practice to have the student use the completed word in a *verbal* sentence.

Directional guidance is also inherent in spelling and writing. They are the other side of the same coin and much practice should be given in all three skills: spelling, writing and reading, reading and more reading.
There is nothing new about the material that we use in teaching blend phonics. It can all be found in "A Guide to Pronunciation" in the front of any dictionary. Take a look at it and you'll say, "Wow, teach that to First graders? Impossible!!" It is not surprising that some anti-phonics persons say that it cannot be done. The trick is to present these seemingly complicated facts in a simplified, streamlined, bare bones version that can be assimilated by a six-year old or younger. There are bound to be

differences of opinion as to the order in which the facts should be presented, and also as to which grapheme/phoneme relationships occur with sufficient frequency to be considered "regular," and which are so rare as to be called "irregular." Even pronunciations may vary due to geographical and ethnic differences.

English is a wondrous and varied means of communication, but at heart it is simple and consistent. In first grade we must teach the *heart* of the subject and not get bogged down with linguistic niceties. In this way we can provide the *basic* tool that a person can develop and expand all through life to enjoy a means of communication to express the most complex thoughts and feelings, and to understand those of fellow human beings.

I found I could provide this tool adequately in its simplest form to my school children in daily half-hour sessions in the first semester of the first grade. By starting in September, children have gained a working knowledge of the 44 phonetic elements in the English language and an overall concept of its basic structure before winter vacation. While their knowledge may not be l00% perfect, it will be sufficient so that they can, with the teacher's continuing help as needed, utilize the phonic key to unlock 85% of the words in the English language. (The other 15%, while largely regular, contain phonetic irregularities which sometimes require a little extra help from the teacher.)

The format of these lessons consists in taking a regular word and building it up phonetically as a class exercise. Then a child is called on to use it in a sentence. At first it is sometimes practically necessary to put the words in the child's mouth until it is understood what is meant by making up a sentence. As soon as the child catches on, the lessons become lively and spirited. The children are eager to participate. (When I inadvertently failed to give a child a turn, I heard about it!)

It was something like "Show and Tell" without the "Show." Instead of using a "Show" object as an inspiration for conversation, we used the key word which we had built up phonetically. Actually it was a language lesson as well as a reading lesson because the children learned to speak in complete, correct sentences. The context was limited only by the children's speaking vocabularies and was not confined to sentences like. "Go. go, run. run, see, see" or like "A fat cat sat on a mat."

I recall one instance when we had sounded out the word "mill." To avoid missing anyone, ordinarily I called on the children in turn, but this time I simply had to break the rule to call on the little fellow who was waving his hand frantically and just bursting to tell us something. He blurted out, "My daddy has a sawmill." Now that's what I call reading with comprehension!

True, we read only one word at a time but it was always phonetically regular and there was no guesswork. By the time we had completed the 47 Units, the children had the feeling of security that comes from knowing that the language was basically an ordered, dependable system. As we came to words in our books that contained irregularities, they were welcomed as something surprising, unique, different and thus easy to remember.

It is possible to teach this work from the chalkboard, but it means that the teacher is half turned away from the class. An overhead projector is ideal because the lighted area holds the children's attention and, since the teacher faces the class directly, there is better control and more eye contact.

As to textbooks with which to implement this study, it would no doubt be easier for the teacher who is using blend phonics for the first time if phonics-based texts were available, correlated more or less with the structured phonics lessons. However, I can vouch from both tutoring and actual classroom experience that any books—old or new—can be used if they are of interest to the children and suitable for their age level. A few problems may be encountered in the first four months if the books have words that contain phonetic elements that have not as yet been introduced in the structured phonics lessons, but it is not too difficult to muddle through this phase. After the children have been exposed to the 44 phonetic elements, they can tackle anything with a little help from their teacher. Frequently, delighted parents reported to me that their children were reading from newspapers and magazines and were devouring library books at a great rate.

In the second semester we used much enrichment material. All of the children belonged to our Book Club. They took home books that they selected during regularly scheduled visits to the school library. My Room Mother arranged to have a volunteer mother sit in the hallway outside the classroom two afternoons a week. The children were excused from the classroom one by one to give brief book reports to the mother who added a star to the child's bookmark for each book read.

Blend Phonics is just about the easiest lesson to teach that can be imagined. No preparation is needed (except to have at hand a copy of the groups of words as given in the LESSON PLANS); no papers to correct for this phase of the reading lesson; no compulsory tests to be given. The children themselves do most of the work by making up sentences, and thus they learn by doing. It's easy; it's inexpensive and it works!

LESSON PLANS FOR THE TEACHING OF

BLEND PHONICS IN FIRST GRADE

Do not delay teaching the names of the letters of the alphabet. They are not only necessary in spelling and in the use of the dictionary, the telephone directory and alphabetical filing systems, but they will help in teaching the sounds. The sounds of many consonants are heard in the letters' names and the long sounds of the vowels **a, e, i, o** and **u*** are identical to their names.

(NOTE: Because the soft sounds of the letters **c** and **g** are heard in these letters' names and thus are easier to teach, we introduce the hard sounds first and provide plenty of opportunity to practice them. Also we make sure the student is familiar with the short sounds of vowels before we present the easy-to-teach long sounds.)

The vowels are **a, e, i, o, u** and sometimes **y**. If a letter is not a vowel, then it is a consonant.

In our first lessons in blend phonics (or word building), we teach the sound of a consonant, then the short sound of a vowel. The child is taught to look at these letters **from left to right** (IMPORTANT) as they are presented to him one by one and as the sound is blended. Then we add another consonant to form a word which the child uses in a verbal sentence to insure comprehension.

It is true that, when we pronounce the sound of a consonant in isolation, it is necessary to add an extraneous neutral (or schwa) sound. This is of no importance because, when the consonant is blended with the vowel, the schwa sound is elided. For example:

b says **b-uh**

a says **ă**

Blend **b-uh** and **ă** to make **bă**

The **uh** sound has disappeared.

u has two long sounds. One is the same as its name; the other is like long **oo.*

The great advantage of this technique is the fact that the child has received directional guidance and has been taught, step by step, to look at the word from **left to right**. This is extremely important because many children have a normal, natural tendency to look at words from right to left. When shown the word as a whole, they may not see what the teacher sees. If shown the word **ten** the child may see **n-e-t**. Such reversals cause serious confusion when the child is shown whole words as is the case in the look-say method which incorporates no detailed directional guidance.

After you make the blend, **ba**, add the letter **t** to form the word **bat**. Have the child make up a verbal sentence using the word **bat**. If necessary, use leading questions to help the child think of a sentence.

For example: TEACHER: If you have a ball, what do you do with the **bat**?

CHILD: I hit the ball with the **bat**.

Use this format to teach each of the words in Unit 1 for the short sound of **a**. Then introduce the short sound of **i** and teach the children to sound out as many of the words given in Unit 2 as are necessary for good practice. Choose the words that will be most interesting to the class and, of course, let **the children take turns using each word in a verbal sentence**. Continue in the same manner with short **o**, short **u** and short **e**. Short **e** may give some difficulty because the sound of this letter is easily confused with the short sound of **i**. (We have all heard some people say "git" or "get" and "ingine" for "engine.")

When teaching this work to an individual, use a chalkboard, slate or paper and pencil. For teaching a class, a chalkboard is adequate but an overhead projector is ideal because the teacher is able to face the class directly.

You will notice that the units, if taught in the order given, are cumulative. That is, only one new phonetic element (or related group of elements) is introduced in grapheme/phoneme relationship(s) plus those that were used in the previous units. The work proceeds step by easy step. It is not obligatory to teach phonics in this particular order, but this presentation is one that has proved successful over the years.

When your students have completed all 47 units they will have been introduced to all of the regular phonetic elements in the English language. They will then have the tools with which they can sound out 85% of all words. Most children will need help in implementing this basic knowledge in actual reading and may need help in identifying the graphemes in a word. For example, when the student comes to the word, **teaching**, it may be necessary to help break it down into its phonetic components: **t-ea-ch-ing**. Often it takes only a quiet hint: (**ea** sounds like long **e**) to give the child the clue needed.

To help students with the 15% of words that contain phonetic irregularities, consult your dictionary. Write the word as it is given in parentheses following the correct spelling in the dictionary. For example, *said* (sed). Although students must learn the correct spelling, they can sound out the word as it is given in parentheses.

Phonetic irregularities occur most frequently in short, commonly used words. As the child reads more advanced material the phonic training will become increasingly useful and the child can achieve independence in reading unfamiliar words.

The basic work should be presented to a class in one semester (Sept.-Dec.) in half-hour periods daily in the first grade. Homeschool parents will complete the Units at a pace that works for their children. Large word lists have been included to demonstrate how the phonics system provides the key to unlock unlimited numbers of words…unlike the narrow capabilities of the "controlled vocabularies" associated with the look-say method.

It is helpful to lay out a schedule at the beginning of the semester, allotting certain time-periods in which to present words from a given number of units. The objective would be to introduce all of the units before winter vacation. Remember that this formal introduction is merely the foundation. It starts the child off right by giving strong directional guidance and an overall understanding of the phonetic structure of the language. **It must be accompanied by—and followed by—much practice in writing and reading of books**.

If one is adapting this material to individual work—rather than a class—it is well to plan on at least 50 hours in which the basic units are supplemented by exercises in writing and practice in reading.

Phonics-based textbooks are useful—especially for those who are teaching phonics for the first time. However, the lack of such textbooks is no excuse for the failure to teach the material in these Lesson Plans. Any sort of book may be used. The writer has done it successfully using the only books at hand: look-say basal readers! When words are encountered which contain sounds that have not as yet been taught in formal phonics lessons, they may be offered as whole words or better still, if the teacher feels up, to it, may be presented as a "preview" of what is to come in the formal sessions.

The writer knows from actual classroom experience that, even though the textbook material is not coordinated with the structured phonics lessons, the problem will solve itself when, in a few weeks' time, the class has completed the 47 units in these Lesson Plans. Don't make a big issue of it. Be patient, pleasant and adaptable during textbook reading lessons but, on the other hand, do not let anything interfere with the daily half-hour formal phonics sessions. At the end of the first semester, with the guidance and assistance of the teacher and with supplementary work in writing and spelling, the children will be able to sound out words in any reading material suitable to their age level.

If millage failures and tight budgets—or the prejudice of school administrators or supervisors—preclude the possibility of new phonics-based textbooks, don't despair. Remember how many persons in history learned to read with only the Bible or Pilgrim's Progress for textbooks and, though Abraham Lincoln never saw a basal reader, he achieved mastery of the English Language.

Do plan a tentative schedule before you begin to teach this material. The 47 units in these Lesson Plans should be completed in about four months. Do not linger over any one unit. Do not expect the student to know perfectly the sound in one unit before you go on to the next. After all, this material is arranged to provide a continuing "built-in" review. For example, if you are teaching the word "toothbrush" in Unit 31, the only new sound is that of long **oo**. The other sounds, **t, th, b, r, u** and **sh** are review elements. When all 47 units have been completed, don't worry if the student has not learned thoroughly every phonetic element that has been presented in this preliminary work. From now on, every time the student reads any written matter whatsoever it will constitute a review of the material in these Lesson Plans. It is to be expected that the student will need help and reminders for some time after the four months of initial instruction is completed. The more practice the student has in reading, the sooner complete mastery of phonic skills will be achieved.

Now you are ready for the first lesson. You have before you groups of words to guide you, but remember that these mere skeletons of your lessons. It is your task to inspire the children to put flesh on the bones and to breathe life into them. Here is a sampling of a proven teaching method.

THE TEACHER SAYS:	THE TEACHER WRITES
The name of this letter is **b**. It says **b-uh**.	b
The name of this letter is **a**. Its short sound is **ă**	a
Blend **b-uh** and ă	ba
Now we'll add the letter **t** that says **t-uh**.	bat
What is the word? (Pronounce it with the class.)	

    CLASS: **bat**

I'll draw a picture of a **bat**.

Johnny, if you have a ball,
what do you do with the **bat**?

    JOHNNY: I hit the ball with the **bat**.

Good, let's sound out another word.
This word also starts with **b** that says **b-uh**.

b

The next letter is **a** that says **ă**.

a

Blend **b-uh** and **ă** together to make **bă**

ba

Now we'll add the letter **g** that says
(hard sound of **g**)

bag

What is the word? (Pronounce the word
bag with the class.) I'll draw a picture of a **bag**.

Mary, in what does you mother carry
groceries home from the store?

> MARY: She carries them home in a **bag**.

That's fine. You have read two words this
morning. Let's sound another word

b says **buh**

b

a says **ă**

a

Blend **b-uh** and **ă** to make **bă.**

ba

Now we'll add **d** that says **d-uh**.
The word is? Class?

bad

> CLASS: **bad**

Billy, a dog walked on mother's clean floor
with muddy paws. Was that good?

> BILLY: No it was **bad**.

(NOTE: If Billy has a dog, he will probably want
to tell about something bad that he did.
Point to – and pronounce – the new word
whenever it is used.)

Now we'll start the next with another letter.   c
It's name is **c** and it has more than one
sound, but today we will learn only the
hard sound**: k-uh**.

You remember **a;** it says **ă**.   a

Blend **k-uh** and **ă** together to make **ca**.   ca

Now we'll add the letter **p** that says **p-uh**.   cap

The word, class, is?

> CLASS: **cap**

Donald, what do you wear on your head?

> DONALD: I wear a **cap**.

Continue in this fashion. After you have finished Unit 1, you need not try to teach all of the words in the longer units. Choose the words you think will be most interesting to the children. Stay on your schedule so that the work will be completed in about four months.

It is important that each child has a turn making up a sentence. This is the "bait" that is used to hold the children's attention. They will not realize that they are sounding out "lists of words" because they will be so intent in expressing their own thoughts as they incorporate the "key" words in sentences.

If anyone is bashful or slow in responding, gently ask leading questions to draw the child out. Don't be afraid to improvise. Talk about the "key" words as much as is needed. Then ask the child to tell **you** something about it even if, at first, the response consists only of a parrot version of your ideas. The children will soon have their own delightful, original sentences. Of course, our purpose is to encourage them to think of the **meaning** of the "key" words. A six-year old child's verbal vocabulary is said to consist of 5,000 - 10,000 words or more. These lessons provide a means of exercising that vocabulary and developing a reading vocabulary at the same time.

CONSONANTS and VOWELS
A SUMMARY of PHONETIC SOUNDS

Our alphabet has 26 letters.

Each **letter** has one **name** and one or more sounds.

The **consonants** are all the letters, except a, e, i, o, u.

Consonants: b, c, d, f, g, h, j, k, l, m, n, p, q, r, s , t, v, w, y, z.

Vowels: a, e, i, o, u and sometimes y (which is sometimes a vowel and sometimes a consonants.)

Most **single consonants** have only one sound.
    Example: the "b" sound you hear in "baby"
    Exceptions: "c" has a **hard sound** "k" (as in "cat") and
        c has a **soft sound** "s" when followed by **e, i,** or **y** (as in "cent, city, fancy")
        "g" has a **hard sound** "g" (as in "go") and sometimes a **soft   sound** "j" when followed by **e, i** or **y** (as in "age, ginger, gym")

In a **consonant blend** you hear the sounds of two or three consonants blended together.
    Example: Single consonant   **r**ap
            Consonant blend with two consonants   **tr**ap
            Consonant blends with three consonants   **str**ap

---

In a **consonant digraph** you do not hear the separate sounds of the consonants, but you do hear a new sound. (Most of the consonant digraphs are a consonant followed by an "h")
    Example: **ch** – church   **th** – that   **ph** – phone
              sh – shop   **wh** – when   **gh** – laugh

98

Some letters are **silent** that is do not have any sound in the word.
   Example: Silent consonant "b" – com*b*. Silent vowel "e" – dat*e*.

Every word has one or more **syllables**. A syllable is a "**beat**" in the word.
This symbol ´ means the syllable is **accented,** or has the **heavy beat**.
   Example: un´der   be gin´   in for ma´ tion

Every syllable has a **vowel sound**. The vowels are a, e, i, o, u, and
sometimes y.
   ("y" is usually a consonant when it is the first letter in the word, as in
"yes," but a vowel when it is in the middle or at the end of, as in "gym"
or "my")

Each vowel has several different sounds, depending on how it is used in
   the word.

A single vowel usually has the **short sound** (˘)
   Example: ădd, ĕxit, ĭt, ŏn, ŭp

A single vowel may have the **long sound** (¯ means long).
   Example: dāte, mē, Ī, gō, ūses

A **closed syllable** ends in a consonant, and the vowel sound is **short.**
   Example: gŏt

An **open syllable** ends in a vowel, and the vowel sound is **long.**
   Example: gō

Silent "e" as the end of the word usually makes the vowel before it **long.**
   Example: āte, Pēte, rīde, hōpe, tŭbe

Often when two vowels come together, the **first one is long** and the
   second one is silent. (The second vowel "works on" the first vowel to
   make it long.)

   Example: ēe – trēe   āi – rāin   īe – pīe   ōa – rōad   ūe – blūe
            ēa – ēat   āy – dāy   ōe – Jōe   ūi – sūit

Two vowels together may give a different sound than those made by the single letter.

They are **digraphs** if they have a single sound.
  Example: oo – m**oo**n   oo – b**oo**k   au – P**au**l

They are **diphthongs** when two sounds slide together to make a continuous unit of sound.
  Example: oi – **oil**   oy – b**oy**   ou – **out**   ow – c**ow**

Other vowel sounds can be made with a **vowel followed by an "r."**
  Example: ar – **car**   or – f**or**   er – h**er**
                                        ir – b**ir**d
                                        ur – t**ur**n

Or vowel sounds can be made with a **vowel followed by a "w."**
  Example: aw – s**aw**   ow – c**ow**   ew – n**ew**
                          ow – sl**ow**
("r" and "w" are "vowel helpers" in the above examples.)

The symbol "ə" stands for the **schwa sound,** which is the sound of the **unaccented short "u."**

Any one of the vowels (a, e, i, o, u) can take the schwa sound.
  Example: **a**bout, **e**lephant, polit**i**cs, eb**o**ny, croc**u**s

---

Other common letter combinations using the vowels are:

ăng – s**ăng**	ănk – b**ănk**	all – b**all**	ōlt – b**ōlt**	īnd – f**īnd**
ĕng – s**ĭng**	ĭnk – p**ĭnk**	alt – s**alt**	ōll – r**ōll**	īld – ch**īld**
ŏng – s**ŏng**	ŏnk – h**ŏnk**	alk – w**alk**	ōld - c**ōld**	
ŭng – s**ŭng**	ŭnk – j**ŭnk**			

---

ti, si, ci can say "sh"   Examples: na**ti**on, ten**si**on, spe**ci**al

This "Summary" is from Hazel Loring's original *Blend Phonics*.

Blend Phonics Stories - Ladder of Decoding Skills

Step	Unit	Sound to Symbol Associations	BF Story
	47	37 Dolch List Words & 3 /zh/ Words	62
Step 6 Advanced Spellings	46	Long Vowels in Open Syllables	60, 61
	45	ed with short e; ed sounds like 'd; ed sounds like 't	59
	44	Final le, tion, sion	58
	43	ph sounds like f	57
	42	se sounds like z	56
	41	Silent k, w, t, b, and l	55
	40	Silent gh, and gh like f	54
	39	Soft sound of g in dge & sometimes before e, i, y.	53
	38	Soft sound of c (before e, i, & y); s like sh (sugar)	52
	37	Phonograms: ul, ull, ush (u sound like short oo)	51
	36	Unaccented a at beginning of words & a without emphasis	50
Step 5 Vowel Digraphs & Diphthongs	35	Diagraphs ew, ue	49
	34	Phonograms: al, all	48
	33	Vowel Digraphs aw, au	47
	32	Short sound of oo	46
	31	Long sound of oo	45
	30	Diphthong: oy, oi	44
	29	Diphthong ou; Digraph ōu, often Irregular	43
	28	Digraph: ōw, Diphthong: ow	41, 42
	27	Vowel Digraph: oa, oe (like long ō)	40
	26	Final Vowel y (ē); Long ī in single syllable words	38, 39
	25	Vowel Digraph ie (long ī and long ē)	36, 37
	24	Vowel Digraph ea (long ē, short ĕ, long ā)	34, 35
	23	Vowel Digraph: ee	33
	22	Vowel Digraph: ai, ay	32
Step 4 R-Controlled Vowels	21	Phonogram er, ir, ur, and sometimes or	30, 31
	20	Phonogram: or	29
	19	Phonogram: ar	28
Step 3 Long Vowels & Etc.	18	Short words ending in long vowels: be, go, he, me, etc.	27
	17	Phonograms - Long Vowels: old, olt, oll, ost,, oth, ild, ind	26
	16	VCE (long vowels) a-e, e-e, i-e, o-e, u-e	22, 23, 24, 25
Step 2 Consonant Blends & Digraphs	15	Short Vowel Compound Words	19, 20, 21
	14	Initial Consonant Blends: br, cr, dr, fr, gr, pr, tr	17, 18
	13	Initial Consonant Blends: bl cl fl gl pl sc sk sl sm sn sp st sw	15, 16
	12	nk (ank, ink, onk, unk)	14
	11	ng (ang, ing, ong, ung)	13
	10	Consonant Digraph: wh	12
	9	Consonant Digraphs: ch, tch (ch = k)	11
	8	Consonant Digraphs: th (voiced); th (unvoiced)	10
	7	Consonant Digraph: sh	9
	6	Final Consonant Blends	8
Step 1 Short Vowels & Consonants	5	Short vowel ĕ	5, 6, 7
	4	Short vowel ŭ	4
	3	Short vowel ŏ	3
	2	Short vowel ī	2
	1	Short vowel ă b c d f g h j k l m n p qu r s t v w y z ck	1

Reading Made Easy with Blend Phonics for First Grade

by Hazel Logan Loring

Table of Contents

Step One: Short Vowels and Consonants

Step Two: Consonant Blends and Digraphs

Step Three: Long Vowels (VCE)

Step Four: R-Controlled Vowels

Unit 19. Phonogram: ar
Unit 20: Phonogram: or
Unit 21: Phonograms: er, ir, ur and sometimes or

Step Five: Vowel Digraphs and Diphthongs

Unit 22. Vowel Digraph: ai, ay
Unit 23. Vowel Digraph: ee
Unit 24: Vowel Digraph: ea (three phonemes: long e, short e, long a)
Unit 25: Vowel Digraph: ie (two phonemes: long i and long e)
Unit 26. Final Vowel y: sound e. Long i in one syllable words.
Unit 27. Vowel Digraph: oa, oe (like long o)
Unit 28. Digraph ow. Diphthong: ow
Unit 29. Diphthong ou: Digraph ou (Often irregular; it can
      sound like short u, short oo, long oo, long o, etc.)
Unit 30. Diphthongs: oy, oi
Unit 31. Long sound of oo
Unit 32. Short sound of oo
Unit 33. Vowel Digraphs: aw, au
Unit 34. Phonograms: al, all
Unit 35. Digraphs: ew, ue

Step Six: Advanced Spelling Patterns

Unit 36. Unaccented a at the beginning of a word. Schwa sound.
      Also the word a when not used for emphasis.
Unit 37. Phonograms: ul, ull, ush (u sound like short oo)
Unit 38. Soft sound of c (before e, i, and y)
      Usually sounds like s: sometimes like sh.
Unit 39. Soft sound of g in dge and sometimes before e, i, and y.
Unit 40. Silent gh and gh sounds like f.
Unit 41. Silent k, w, t, b, l, and h.
Unit 42. se sounds like z
Unit 43. ph sounds like f
Unit 44. Final le, tion, sion
Unit 45. ed with short e; ed sounds like 'd, ed sounds like 't
Unit 46. Long Vowels in Open Syllables
Unit 47. 37 word Dolch Words and 3 words with the /zh/ sound

The *Table of Contents* was prepared by Donald L. Potter – June 2003. Final revision 5/24/17.

Blend Phonics Progress Chart

Student: _____ Teacher: _____

School: _____ Begin Date _____ Ending Date_____

1. Sam, a cat Unit 1: **Step 1**	2. A Tin Can Unit 2	3. A Mop Unit 3	4. A Bug Unit 4	5. A Wet Hen Unit 5	6. A Pug Unit 5
7. A Fox Unit 5	8. A Lamp Unit 6: **Step 2**	9. Ship on a Shelf Unit 7	10. The Thump Unit 8	11. The Chick Unit 9	12. The Whisk Unit 10
13. Sing a Song Unit 11	14. The Tank Unit 12:	15. The Flag Unit 13	16. The Sled Unit 13	17. The Brass Band Unit 14	18. The Frog Unit 14
19. Yuck & Yum Unit 15	20. The Hilltop Unit 15	21. Handstands Unit 15	22. Cakes Unit 16: **Step 3**	23. The Kite Unit 16	24. Pine Cones Unit 16
25. The Rude Duke Unit 16	26. The Cold Unit 17	27. Go! Unit 18	28. The Car Unit 19: **Step 4**	29. Morning on the Farm Unit 20	30. The World Unit 21
31. Can I be? Unit 21	32. A Fine Day Unit 22 **Step 5**	33. A Bee Unit 23	34. The Sea Unit 24	35. Bread of Life Unit 24	36. Pie Unit 25
37. The Chief Priest Unit 25	38. Sunny Day Unit 26	39. The Fly Unit 26	40. Goat and Toad Unit 27	41. The Fish Bowl Unit 28	42. Brown Cow Unit 29
43. A Mouse Unit 29	44. Boys Unit 30	45. Loose Stoop Unit 31	46. A Good Book Unit 32	47. Dawn Unit 33	48. A Ball Unit 34
49. Stew Unit 35	50. Asleep Unit 36: **Step 6**	51. The Bush Unit 37	52. The Circus Unit 38	53. The Stage Unit 39	54. The Flight Unit 40
55. The Knight Unit 41	56. Cheese Please! Unit 42	57. The Elephant Unit 43	58. My Mission Unit 44	59. Finished Unit 45	60. The Slimy Spider Unit 46.
61. The Giant Ruin Unit 46	62. The Treasure Hunt Unit 47				

Six Steps to Reading Success:

Step-One: Short vowels and Consonants   **Step-Four**: R-Controlled Vowels
Step-Two: Consonant Blends & Digraphs   **Step-Five**: Vowel Digraphs & Diphthongs
Step-Three: Long Vowel (VCE) Diphthongs   **Step-Six**: Advanced Spellings

Copyright © 2012 by Donald L. Potter. Revised 7/20/2017.

Characteristics of Fluent Performance
The Goal of Blend Phonics Reading Instruction

Fluent performance is characterized by (1) the ability to perform a skill or recall knowledge long after formal learning programs have ended, (2) the ability to maintain performance levels and attention to tasks for extended periods while resisting distraction, and (3) the ability to combine and apply what is learned to perform more complex skills, creatively, and in new situations. ("Fluency: Achieving True Mastery in the Learning Process" by Carl Binder, Elizabeth Haughton, and Barbara Bateman (2002).

Concerning Spelling

Spelling is the flip side of reading. A good speller is generally a good reader. Ronald P. Carver (*Causes of High and Low Reading Achievement,* 2000) reminds us that spelling was used to teach reading for over 200 years. The current neglect of spelling explains to a large degree the inordinate amount of illiteracy in America today. The spelling is a central feature of the *Blend Phonics* program and should not be neglected. Letter names are taught from the start of the program so the students can practice oral spelling with the very first unit.

Isabel L. Beck Explains the Advantage of the Blend Phonics Technique

In contrast to final blending, I strongly recommend **successive blending** (which I have sometimes called **cumulative blending**). In **successive blending**, students say the first two sounds in a word and immediately blend those two sounds together. They say the third sound and immediately blend that with the first two blended sounds. If it is a four-phoneme word, then they say the fourth phoneme and immediately blend that with the first three blended sounds. The strong advantage of **successive blending** is that it is less taxing on the short-term memory because blending occurs immediately after each new phoneme is pronounced. As such, at no time must more than two sounds be held in memory (the sound immediately proceed and the one that directly precedes it), and at no time must more than two sound units be blended (50) A strong advantage of the **successive blending chain** is the precise information available to the teacher in locating an error. If a child makes an error while performing the chain, the teacher knows where the error is - that is, which link in the chain is incorrect. With this kind of precise information, the teacher can give the child a direct prompt... The availability of precise information enables the teacher to go right into where the problems is and deal with it. This is in contrast to simply knowing that a child didn't read *black* or *set* correctly (53, 54). *Making Sense of Phonics: The Hows and Whys.* 1st ed.

Dr. George Gonzalez' Eight Comprehension Skills

<u>Five Literal Comprehension Skills</u> (Right there on the page.)

1. Recall Facts & Details.

2. Distinguish Fact & Opinion

3. Recall Sequence of Events

4. Identify Cause and Effect

5. Main Idea: Who? Did what? Where? When? Why?

<u>Three Inferential Comprehension Skills</u> (In the student's head, not on the page.)

6. Predict Outcome

   Key Questions: (1) What is going to happen next? (2) What is ___ going to do now? (3) Where is ___ going? (4) Who is going to be there? (5) How is __ going to feel? (6) What is ___ going to say? (7) What is ___ going to think? (8) What is going to be found there? (9) Who is going to win at the end? (10) How are they (we) going to solve the problem?

7. Draw Conclusions

   Key Questions: (1) What seems to be happening? (2) How would you explain this? Why do you think this happens? (3) What could have gone wrong? What would you have done? (4) How do you feel about this? How would you have felt? (5) Why do you say this? (6) Why do you feel this way? (7) What is your opinion? Who is Right? Who is wrong? (8) Whose side are you on? Who do you like? Dislike? (9) Who do you think is right? Do you agree? Disagree? (10) What else is possible. What information is needed?

8. Generalization

   Key Questions: (1) What can we learn from this story? (2) What is the story trying to teach us? (3) What is the story trying to teach us? (4) What is the moral of the story? (5) What is the message of the story? (6) What is the argument presented in this article? (7) What is the importance of the story? (8) What is the story really about? (9) What is the story implying? What are the implications of the article? (10) What is the generalization found in the experiment. What is the theorem operating in the problem?

These skills were used to construct the comprehension questions for the *Blend Phonics Lessons and Stories.* Dr. George González was a Professor of Bilingual Education/ESL/Bicultural Studies at the University of Texas/Pan American, Edinburg, TX.

ABOUT THE AUTHOR

Mr. Donald L. Potter has been teaching beginning and remedial reading for over thirty years. He subbed full time for all subjects and grade levels for five years before becoming a certified teacher. He was a public school teacher for the Ector County ISD in Odessa Texas for twenty-one years, teaching elementary bilingual, secondary Spanish, Amateur Radio (NG5W), and dyslexia classes.

He taught for from 2006 to 2019 at the Odessa Christian School. While there, he taught numerous subjects including elementary and middle school Spanish, cursive handwriting for all grades, remedial reading (dyslexia), manuscript handwriting, Middle School Bible, computers, 7th grade Texas history, 8th grade American history, 3rd grade history, English grammar, spelling and regular 4th grade. He resigned from the Christian School on May 31, 2019 to dedicate his time to tutoring and educational consulting with schools.

In the evenings after school and during summer vacation, he tutors students of all ages who have reading problems. He, also, is available to do reading and handwriting workshops for schools, colleges, and homeschool parents.

He has been publishing on the Internet since 2003. His website, www.donpotter.net, is a rich resource for educators looking for workable solutions to reducing the high illiteracy rates in America.

He is the sponsor of *The Blend Phonics Nationwide Educational Reform Campaign* at www.blendphonics.org. This Campaign is based on the highly effective *Blend Phonics* approach published by Mrs. Hazel Logan Loring in 1980. Thousand of teachers have found this to be one of the most effective and easiest-to-teach methods ever published.

He is also an experienced handwriting teacher. His *Shortcut to Manuscript* and *Shortcut to Cursive* are available for free from his website. He has used both systems successful with students from kindergarten through adult. Fluent handwriting (coupling speed and legibility) is a **necessary foundation** for fluent reading and accurate spelling.

Made in the USA
Las Vegas, NV
06 November 2022

58947342R00066